The Futura Library of Comic Speeches

SALES FORCE

4. Comic Speeches for the Sales Force

Also from Futura:

THE FUTURA LIBRARY OF COMIC SPEECHES

1. COMIC SPEECHES FOR SPORTSMEN
2. COMIC SPEECHES FOR SOCIAL OCCASIONS
3. COMIC SPEECHES FOR THE LEGAL PROFESSION

The Futura Library of Comic Speeches

SALES FORCE

4. Comic Speeches for the Sales Force

Futura

A Futura Book

First published in Great Britain in 1986
by Futura Publications, A Division of
Macdonald & Co (Publishers) Ltd
London & Sydney

ISBN 0 7088 2988 0

Typeset by Leaper & Gard Ltd, Bristol, England
Printed and bound in Great Britain by
William Collins, Glasgow

Futura Publications
A Division of
Macdonald & Co (Publishers) Ltd
Greater London House
Hampstead Road
London NW1 7QX
A BPCC plc Company

Contents

PART ONE

How to make a comic speech

Ground Rules

Salesmen have a great advantage when it comes to making speeches, and that's because they're used to selling. What, you might ask, does a career spent selling cars or pharmaceuticals have in common with standing up in front of an audience and making them laugh? The connection is that the public speaker has to sell *himself* to his audience, just as the salesman has to sell his goods to his customer.

The very best salesmen have the gift of the gab; the others have to learn to speak persuasively — and so does the public speaker. Natural-born salesmen have an inbuilt way of sizing up customers and responding to them; the rest of us have to learn the technique — and so does the public speaker.

The similarities go even further. Every salesman worth his salt decides his goals in advance and aims to achieve them, knowing that before he can pull off a deal a lot of forward-planning and preparation has to be done. And his main aim is to leave his customer feeling pleased and satisfied with his purchase. All this the public speaker must do too!

To help you, this book contains everything needed to turn a salesman into a public speaker. In it you'll find all the information required to prepare and deliver an entertaining speech — everything from how to assess what kind of material your audience will enjoy to coping with your nerves on the day. And because this is the *complete* guide to comic speechmaking, you'll find hundreds of jokes, anecdotes and quotations to ensure that you're never at a loss for words.

Know your audience

Everyone feels nervous at the mere idea of making a speech to an audience of strangers, but one of the first things you can do to make yourself feel better about it is to realise that nerves are a good thing. Don't just try to ignore them — they won't go away. Instead, resolve to channel all that nervous energy into preparing yourself and your speech so that you please the audience. And the best way of pleasing them, as any salesman knows, is by giving them something they want.

But what *do* they want? That's the fundamental question and one you'll have to answer before you can begin to prepare yourself. Most importantly, every audience wants to hear a speech which has been created especially for them and the occasion, one that is relevant and interesting — to *them.* In a word, it must be entertaining.

There are quite a few public speakers around who, having written one speech, decide to make it do for the rest of their lives and for every occasion at which they're invited to talk. If they're feeling generous they add a few topical jokes or stories, but more often than not they just ramble over tried, trusted and tedious ground. You probably first encountered one of this breed at a school speech day and there's usually one at weddings and company dinners. They even pop up on television these days, appearing on three chat shows in a single week and telling the same stories on them all!

Even worse than this kind of speaker, there's the one who imagines himself to be such a naturally gifted orator that he doesn't prepare any material at all. Admittedly there are a few people who can make brilliant impromptu speeches; they tend to be rich and famous because it's such a rare gift. Those who don't have it simply drone on for as long as the fancy takes them, usually until their guests are about to pass out from boredom. Such speakers enjoy themselves, but they don't please their audiences — and pleasing your audience is the very first rule of speech-making.

The audience

Before you can start working out how to please them, you'll have to find out about them. Will they appreciate your slightly risqué stories about life as a travelling salesman, or would they prefer to hear something a little more sedate? Remember, it's the audience who will decide whether your material is funny or not. You may find it hilarious, but if *they* don't you might just as well give up. So before you do anything else, assess your audience and decide on the right kind of material for them.

Age is an important factor. A young and sophisticated audience will respond to a different kind of material than an older gathering. An audience composed of fellow sales personnel will enjoy jokes and stories that might be lost on the local Ladies Circle. Bear this in mind when you come to select your material.

Also bear in mind the sex of your audience. The kind of jokes guaranteed to go down a bomb at an all-male sales office celebration will go down less well in mixed company, so be careful. In fact it's always best to avoid dirty jokes altogether, particularly if you're in a work situation. If you embarrass strangers you at least have the comfort of knowing that you're unlikely to meet them again. The same can't be said if you upset your colleagues.

Find out from the organisers of the occasion as much information as you can — about the people on the committee, if there is one, the names and interests of any special guests, the aims of the organisation and about any other speakers and what they'll be talking on. Then do some homework to see if you can come up with any amusing stories that will tie in perfectly with the occasion — make them the basis of your speech. This may sound like unnecessarily hard work, but some topical and personal references can make all the difference between a passable and a brilliant speech. They prove that you've cared enough to do some research — and as all salesmen know, there's nothing that a customer responds to more warmly than some personal interest.

The occasion

Different occasions require different kinds of speeches. You'll find guidelines on the kind of speech to make at conferences, presentations, dinners and various functions in the last part of this section. Remember, though, that it isn't just the formal requirements of an occasion that matter. Tone is important, too, and you must anticipate and be sensitive to it. A skilled salesman judges the mood of his customer and responds to it, and so must the public speaker. What kind of entertainment is your audience expecting? A boozy evening function demands a robust kind of humour. A lunchtime speaking engagement may be more subdued and require a wittier approach. A retirement presentation may call for a gentle, nostalgic tone, while a funny speech urging the sales force on to even greater achievements might benefit from a punchy, aggressive feel. Use your judgement and bear the mood of the occasion in mind when you're selecting your material.

If you've been invited to propose a toast or make a presentation, make sure you do so — don't get carried away and forget what you're there for. At a recent dinner the speaker, who was supposed to present an award to the company's best salesman, got so absorbed in what he had to say that he sat down still holding the award and had to be reminded by the chairman that it wasn't his to keep! The best way of avoiding this kind of embarrassment is to plan your speech well in advance and stick to it. Try to resist the temptation to improvise, no matter how well you're received, because it's improvisation that's likely to throw you off your stride.

Here's a check list of 10 simple Do's and Don't's which you should bear in mind as you sit down to prepare your speech.

Do's

1. Do aim to entertain and please your audience.
2. Do some research beforehand, paying particular attention to the age and sex of your audience.
3. Do find out about your role. Are you to present an award or make a toast? Make sure that you prepare the right kind of speech.
4. Do find out about any special guests or facts and refer to them in your speech.
5. Do choose the right kind of material for the occasion.

Don't's

1. Don't use old material.
2. Don't risk offending anyone with blue jokes.
3. Don't include irrelevant material that will bore your audience.
4. Don't forget to fulfil your function, be it proposing a toast or offering a vote of thanks.
5. Don't improvise or speak for too long.

Perfect Preparation

Once you know the kind of speech you're going to make and the sort of audience you'll be entertaining, you can begin to prepare your material. Preparation is absolutely vital if you're going to give a polished performance, so allow as much time as possible to work on the speech.

Start by reading through this book and jotting down all the jokes, quotes, anecdotes and so on that you like and that you feel are directly relevant to your audience. Be ruthless and cut out anything that isn't related in some way to your subject and anything that can't be adapted to fit. On a separate sheet, put down all the things that you *have* to say in the speech and all the points that you particularly want to make.

With any luck you'll begin to see the material falling into place, with the quotes leading into the points you want to make and the stories illustrating the theme. This is exactly what you're aiming for — a seamless speech with one idea moving into the next without any effort. You'll probably have to adapt some of the material if it's to fit in perfectly, so change the names and locations and details to suit the occasion. For example, if you're going to be speaking in Newcastle and you're using a joke set in London, change the location and add some Geordie colour. Most importantly of all, put everything into your own words. You'll feel more comfortable when you come to use the material if it's written in the kind of language and the style you're used to, and it will make your speech seem that much more personal to the audience.

Sir Thomas Beecham once said of his orchestra that the important thing was 'to begin and end together, what happens in between doesn't matter very much.' Pretty much the same can be said of making a speech. If you can capture the attention of the audience with your first line, you're likely to have them with you for the rest of the speech. And if they're going to remember anything when they get home, it's likely to be your final line — so make sure that it's worth remembering.

Some speakers like to work on the opening and closing lines of their speech together, linking them so that the last line finishes what the first line started. Whatever you decide to do, make sure that both the beginning and the end of your speech are absolutely relevant — both to the occasion and the central part of the speech. Nothing irrelevant should be allowed in at all or you'll begin to look as if you're rambling.

Opening and closing a speech are the two most difficult things of all. Try using one of these opening gambits.

Quotations

You'll find dozens of useful quotations in this book and one of them should be ideal for opening your speech. When you're looking for it, bear in mind that it should allow you to move straight into the main part of your speech without any stress. If you have to force a quotation to fit your theme then forget it. Always inform your audience that it *is* a quote and not your own words. It's quite likely that someone in the audience will have heard it before and they might think you a fraud if you don't name the person who said it first.

Don't use a quotation for the opening *and* closing of your speech because that would look too much like cheating, but a quote can round off a speech perfectly. Again, you'll find something suitable in the relevant section of this book — and again, make sure that it ties in completely with the main subject of your speech.

Questions

A question can be a very effective way of getting your speech off the ground. Try asking an apparently serious one and following it up with a ridiculous answer. Or ask a ridiculous question to which there's no answer. Whichever kind you choose, aim to raise a laugh from the audience and break the ice.

The 'Did you know?' gambit is also a useful one. Find an amazing fact in the relevant section of this book and ask your audience if they knew it. It's bound to start your speech off with a bang!

Jokes

A joke may seem the obvious way of starting a speech, but in fact jokes can go badly wrong. If they work you'll have the audience eating out of your hand — but if they fall flat you'll have everyone in an agony of embarrassment and praying that you finish quickly.

The best kind of joke to look out for is one that has something to do with a member of the audience or with something directly relevant to the occasion. You may find that simply by changing a few details in one of the jokes in this book you've got the ideal opening gag — in which case use it. But never use a joke simply because you think it's funny.

Exactly the same advice can be applied to ending a speech. No speech, no matter how well-received, can be counted a great success unless it ends on a high note. Looking for a new screenplay, Sam Goldwyn once remarked, 'What we want is a story that begins with an earthquake and builds up to a climax.' That's what you have to aim for too!

Never end with an apologetic, 'Well, folks, that's about it,' line. That only suggests that you've run out of ideas or that you couldn't be bothered to finish the job off properly, and there's really no excuse for that. Even if you can't find the kind of climax that Goldwyn was looking for, you can end your speech in an amusing and tidy way.

Anecdotes

There's bound to be an anecdote in this book that will encapsulate and illustrate your theme perfectly. You can use it to finish your speech in classic style, but beware of using anything too long or rambling. You don't want to lose your audience's attention in the last few moments. If you're speaking about friends, family or colleagues at work, try to uncover an amusing story about them; nothing embarrassing, of course, just something to show what nice people they are. This is *guaranteed* to bring your speech to a successful conclusion.

Jokes

Ending a speech with a joke is even more risky than opening with one. After all, even if your opening joke falls flat you have the rest of your speech to regain the audience's interest. If you end with a damp squib, no matter how good the speech the audience will remember you for only one thing — your failure to pull it off. Only finish with a joke if you can think of nothing better and if you're absolutely certain that it will work.

When you're preparing your speech, take an occasional look at this checklist of 10 Do's and Don't's just to keep your aims in mind.

Do's

1 Do check your material to ensure that it's suitable for the audience you assessed in the last section.
2 Do make sure that you have included all the things you *have* to say — your vote of thanks or the toast, for example.
3 Do adapt all the material to ensure that it's relevant.
4 Do aim to start and finish your speech on a high note.
5 Do credit any quotations you use.

Don't's

1 Don't use any material that isn't relevant to the occasion or will cause offence.
2 Don't start your speech with a joke unless you feel confident that it will work.
3 Don't tail off at the end of the speech; finish properly.
4 Don't use too many quotes or anecdotes from the lives of other people.
5 Don't speak too long; make sure that your speech is the right length.

If, when you finish preparing your speech, you feel confident that you've observed these guidelines, you can be sure that you're halfway towards success. Now all you need to know is how to deliver the speech you've written!

Successful Delivery

Preparing your speech is one thing — and the most important of all — but delivering it is something else. The best speech can be ruined by poor delivery and the thoroughly mediocre made to pass muster by good technique. Fortunately just a few simple measures will ensure that your delivery does your speech justice.

Rehearsal

You don't need to learn your material like an actor, but rehearsal will help you to become familiar with it and iron out any problems that weren't apparent on paper. For example, you may find that a particular sequence of words turn out to be difficult to say, or you might have problems pronouncing certain words — in which case rewrite them. Try to learn half a dozen key phrases which will take you smoothly from one part of your speech to the next so that you don't keep having to refer to your notes; no matter how nervous you're feeling, this will make your speech seem smooth and practised.

While you're rehearsing, experiment by using your voice to emphasise different points of the speech. Try changing your tone and volume, too, for effect. If you have a tape recorder then use it to tape the various versions of your speech — then you can play them back and decide which sounds the most interesting and lively. Don't, by the way, worry about your accent. Lots of speakers try to iron out their natural accent, but they forget that the way they speak is all part of their personality. Without it they seem very dull. As you listen to yourself speaking you'll begin to recognise the most successful ways of delivering certain parts of your speech. For example, the best way of telling your jokes is to do it casually, without labouring them too much. If you feel that there's a rather dull patch in the speech try animating it by changing your tone or emphasis, or even just speeding it up a bit. It's this kind of preparation that will give you polish on the day.

Body language

No matter how nervous you feel about speaking in front of an audience, you should try not to let them know — and it's the body which most often gives the secret away.

Begin by standing easily with your weight on both feet so that you feel balanced This way you'll look steady, even if you don't feel it. Your main problem will be what to do with your hands. If you have notes, hold them in front of you at about waist level with one hand. With your free hand, lightly grasp the note-holding wrist. If you're lucky, there will be a lectern of some sort at which you can stand. Rest your hands on either side of it and you'll look very much at ease. Only royalty can get away with holding their hands behind their backs, and you'll look sloppy if you put your hands in your pockets, so don't adopt either of these postures. If you've no notes and no lectern, just stand with your left hand lightly holding your right wrist in front of you. It looks surprisingly natural and relaxed. Next time you switch on the TV you'll notice how many presenters and comedians use the position!

Notes

The very worst thing you can do is *read* your speech. Comic speeches need a touch of spontaneity, even if they've been prepared weeks in advance and you've been rehearsing for days. Reading a speech kills it dead. It makes the material seem dull, even if it isn't, it prevents eye contact, which is very important in breaking down the barrier between speaker and audience; and it destroys that important sense of a shared occasion, with speaker and audience responding to each other. On top of all that, the very fact that you are reading will indicate a lack of confidence — and your audience will be alerted to your discomfort and share in it.

That said, it's equally inadvisable to stand up and speak without the aid of any notes at all. Nerves can affect the memories of even professional speakers, so don't take any risks. Many people like to write their notes on postcards, using a single main heading and a couple of key phrases to prompt them. If you decide to do this, make sure that you number the cards clearly. You are bound to drop them if you don't, and reassembling them in the wrong order could create all kinds of chaos! Make sure, too, that you write your headings in large capital letters. When you're standing up and holding the cards at waist level you need to take in all the information at a single glance.

If cards seem too fiddly, write the main headings of your speech on a single sheet of paper, again using a few key words underneath to jog your memory. You'll know, from your rehearsals, those things you find difficult to remember and those which come easily. Jot down the points you get stuck on.

If you're going to use quotations then write them clearly on postcards and read them when the time comes. This ensures that you get them absolutely right and, far from doubting your competence, your audience will be impressed by your thoroughness.

Don't try to hide your notes. Simply use them as

inconspicuously as possible. They prove that you have prepared a speech specially for the occasion and that you care about getting it right — and there's no need to be concerned about that.

On the day

On the day of your speech there are a number of simple precautions you can take to ensure that everything goes smoothly. Some of them may seem quite painfully obvious, but it's the most obvious things that are overlooked, particularly when you're nervous.

Electronic assistance — in the form of microphones and public address systems — needs handling with care. When you accept an invitation to speak, enquire if a microphone is to be provided. If it is, test it before the other guests arrive so that you don't have the embarrassing experience of opening your speech to find that the equipment isn't working. Make a point of checking how to raise or lower the microphone so that if the previous speaker was a giant or a midget you can readjust it without fuss, and try it out, so that you know how far away from it you need to stand. Microphones have a life of their own. You will have to speak directly into some, while others pick up sounds from several feet away. Find out which variety yours is *before* you get to your feet.

If the microphone squeals at you, or despite your preparation, booms too loudly or not at all, get it adjusted during your preliminary remarks, and wait, if necessary, until the fault has been corrected. It may seem amusing to begin with, but the audience will soon tire of it and you won't have a chance to communicate your humour and ideas if they are unable to hear what you have to say or are in constant danger of being deafened.

If you know that you tend to put your hands in your pockets while you're speaking, remove all your loose change and keys so that you're not tempted to jangle them. And make sure that you have a clean handkerchief somewhere about you. A scrap of well-used tissue isn't going to impress the audience when you need to blow your nose.

If you've worked hard to make the opening words of your speech interesting and funny, it would be a great shame to waste them by starting to speak while the audience is still talking and settling down in their seats. So wait for silence, even if it seems to take an age, and when you've obtained it start confidently and loudly so that everyone can hear what you have to say. Whatever you do, don't be hurried. Public speakers talk quite slowly and allow plenty of pauses so that the audience can respond. Take it at a leisurely pace, making sure that you're heard throughout the room, and you'll win the audience's attention immediately.

Some people, but only a very few, are at their best after a few drinks. Unless you know for certain that alcohol will improve your performance, it's probably best not to drink before you speak. Drinking tends to dull reactions and instil a false sense of confidence — and you need to be completely in control of yourself and your material if you're going to make a success of the occasion. Naturally, once you've made your speech and it's been greeted with applause and laughter, you can reward yourself!

Whether you've been drinking or not, accidents do happen. Cope with them by acknowledging them and turning them to your advantage. For example, the speaker who knocked a glass of water over himself brought the house down with the throwaway line, 'Whoops! For a moment there I thought my trousers were on fire!' If someone in the audience drops a glass or falls off their chair, acknowledge it and pause for laughter rather than ploughing on as if nothing has happened. Although you have prepared your speech in advance, you should be aware of things happening around you and flexible enough to add a topical observation or funny remark if necessary. And the better-rehearsed and more at ease you are with your material, the more confident you'll be about including the odd spontaneous line.

If you follow these guidelines you really can't go far wrong. But here, as a last-minute reminder, is a checklist of Do's and Don't's that will ensure that your delivery will do justice to all the work you've put into your speech.

Do's

1. Do rehearse your material.
2. Do work on your posture so that you look relaxed and comfortable.
3. Do prepare your notes and quotations carefully.
4. Do take simple precautions — like dressing correctly, checking microphones and checking your appearance.
5. Do anticipate any accidents and interruptions and be prepared for them.

Don't's

1. Don't read your speech.
2. Don't make any last-minute attempts to change your accent or your appearance.
3. Don't arrive late or unprepared.
4. Don't start your speech before everyone is ready.
5. Don't drink before you make your speech.

The Right Speech for the Right Occasion

Every speech you make should be created especially for the occasion — and every occasion requires a different kind of speech. Some occasions are informal, in which case you must use your discretion to decide what will be most appropriate. For most formal occasions, however, there are basic guidelines which it's best to observe, particularly if you don't have much speaking experience. They'll help you to avoid the worst pitfalls and, at the very least, ensure that you make the right kind of speech.

After-dinner speeches

It's quite an honour to be invited to make an after-dinner speech, because it indicates that your host has confidence in your ability to entertain the audience. That said, after-dinner speechmaking strikes terror into the hearts of many speakers.

It's certainly true that standing up on your own and speaking confidently and amusingly to an audience which has very high expectations of you *can* be quite an ordeal, but there are ways of ensuring that your speech is a great success. And the first is preparation. Most wise after-dinner speakers talk for between ten and twenty minutes, and if you're not well prepared it's impossible to be entertaining for that length of time. Preparation will also give you the advantage of seeming spontaneous and at ease, no matter how you're actually feeling inside. Don't underestimate the importance of appearances, because a tense, nervous speaker can't expect to win the confidence of those listening to him. If you look as if you're enjoying yourself you're halfway to persuading the audience that you *are*.

Some very successful speakers are renowned for writing their speeches on the back of an envelope a few minutes before they are introduced to the audience. Don't try to copy them. Others have — which is why in certain circles the audience dread the after-dinner speeches even more than the speakers themselves! Above all else, be entertaining. You may have deeply held views on serious subjects but an after-dinner speech is not the best time to expand on them. Keep your material witty and light and try to pace it so that any longer stories are followed by some quick laughs.

Try also to be brief. When you are first invited to speak, find out from the organisers how long they expect you to speak for and don't exceed it by so much as a minute. It's far better to be brief and wickedly amusing than to speak for half an hour with only a few laughs. Remember that no one ever complained of a speech being too short.

If by any chance you should find that you're not being well received — though if you follow these guidelines that shouldn't happen — the best thing to do is retire gracefully. Condense your argument, get to the conclusion of your speech and sit down with your head held high. There's no point in prolonging everyone's agony.

Conferences and conventions

Humour is a vital ingredient for conferences and conventions, particularly if you're one of the last speakers at an all-day or even days-long gathering. No matter how serious your topic, a joke or amusing quotation will help to capture your audience's attention, and once you have their interest it will be easier to keep it.

If you know that you're going to be one of the last people to speak, bend one of the major guidelines of the earlier section of this book and *don't* prepare your material too thoroughly. If you're very unlucky you may find that the earlier speeches have effectively covered all that you had planned to say in your own address. It's better, in this situation, to be prepared with a good general outline — one with plenty of relevant humour and wit (because that's what will be required at the end of a long day's speeches) — and build on it as the conference progresses. Listen to the other speakers, making a note of their argument and the things you disagree with or strongly approve of. Insert all these points in your outline to prove that you've been listening, and in this way you'll ensure that your speech is completely integrated and relevant.

Energy and enthusiasm are both important on these kinds of occasion. Be positive and amusing; give people what they want to hear but also give them some food for thought. Above all, try not to look on it as too much of an ordeal. It's in fact an opportunity for you to impress fellow members of the sales force and to make your mark on the occasion.

Presentations

Presentations follow a simple formula that can be adapted for all kinds of occasions, from retirements to award ceremonies. The most important thing to include is information, so that the people watching will be able to appreciate what's going on. You can highlight your speech with a joke or an anecdote, but speak for five minutes at the most and try not to steal the show from the person being honoured.

Here's the basic presentation formula being used for an award presentation:

1 *Name the award and give full details about it*
We're here tonight to witness the presentation of the 1986 Golden Lemon award. As you may know, the Golden Lemon is awarded each year by the Lemon Aid Foundation to the member of the sales force who has done the most to promote the image of citrus fruit during the past twelve months. As well as this wonderful Golden Lemon trophy the salesman or woman also receives a cash prize of £1,000 as a reward for their efforts.

2 *State the name of the recipient and what he or she has done to win the award.*
Pippa Passmore is this year's winner, and the news will come as no surprise to those who work with her. It was Pippa who devised our latest sales strategy, which has been a resounding success and has revitalised the image of citrus fruit.

3 *Present the award.*
I'm very pleased, Pippa, to be able to present you with the 1986 Golden Lemon trophy and this cheque for £1,000.

If you ever find yourself in the lucky position of receiving an award, this is the pattern that your answer should follow:

1 *Say thank you to the person making the award and to the organisation he or she represents.*
I'd like to express my thanks both to Mr Jones and to the Lemon Aid Foundation for this lovely award.

2 *Say what the award means to you and what you'll do with it.*
I'm very proud to have been chosen to receive this honour. I shall keep the trophy on my desk so that it will urge me on to even greater efforts next year.

Don't be tempted to go into great detail about all the teamwork and effort that went into your career or award; it's likely to bore people. Also resist the temptation to be modest and say that you can't think what you've done to deserve the honour. Accept it with good grace and be as amusing and brief as you can.

Toasts

If you find yourself asked to propose a toast at a light-hearted and informal occasion, a few witty words often go down well. Two minutes is the optimum length for a toast, so jokes are not in order. You may find that you can adapt a one-liner from the last section of this book to make an appropriate toast for the sales force, but whatever you end up doing, make sure that everything you say is relevant, amusing and leads up to your main purpose — that of encouraging people to raise their glasses.

These guidelines should ensure that you make the right kind of speech at most formal occasions. If, however, you are invited to speak on an occasion that is not dealt with here, find out from the organisers exactly what they require of you and try to give it to them.

This is a final checklist of Do's and Don't's to be considered when you're working out what kind of speech to make on a particular occasion.

Do's

1. Do assess the audience and the formal requirements of the occasion.
2. Find out how long you will be expected to speak for and on which subject.
3. Are you expected to propose a toast or fulfil a function of some kind?
4. Do your research.
5. Do it *now*!

Don't's

1. Don't leave anything to the last minute.
2. Don't leave out a vital part of the proceedings.

Make sure you know what you'll be expected to do.

3 Don't forget to rehearse your material when you have prepared it.
4 Don't try to revamp an old speech; start something completely new.
5 Don't forget to include your thanks and acknowledgements.

PART TWO
The material

Just Jokes

You'll find a joke suitable for every sales-oriented occasion here. Remember that once you've chosen something suitable you'll need to adapt it by adding your own details and observations. That way the joke won't be one you've borrowed from a book, but your own.

A husband came storming home to his wife. 'I was in the pub,' he said, 'and got talking to a door-to-door salesman who's been down this road. He said he'd seduced every woman in the street except one.'

His wife thought for a moment. 'I bet it's that snooty cow at number eight,' she said.

'I hope these sheets are clean,' said a travelling salesman who had spent the last couple of nights in extremely seedy lodgings.

'Of course they are!' protested the landlady. 'I washed them myself. If you don't believe me, feel them. They're still damp.'

A certain travelling salesman had made his reputation by taking his dog with him on calls. One day one of his customers asked him why the dog always accompanied him.

'He talks to me during my journeys,' he said. The customer refused to believe this.

'I'll give you odds of ten to one that you can't make that dog talk,' he laughed. The salesman got down on his hands and knees and tried to coax the dog to talk, but nothing happened. Shrugging, the salesman handed over his money and he and his dog left the premises.

'Why the hell didn't you say something?' he demanded as soon as they were outside.

The dog winked. 'Think of the kind of odds you'll get next time.'

The salesman was spreading something in the middle of the road. 'What on earth do you think you're doing?' said a passing policeman.

'I'm just spreading alligator powder,' said the salesman.

'But there aren't any alligators around here,' said the policeman.

'Which just proves how well it works. Want to buy some?'

The Irish salesman was accompanied on his rounds by a trainee. They stopped for lunch and both took out their sandwiches. The salesman took the top one and his face fell. 'Cheese and pickle,' he said. He looked at the second one. 'More cheese and pickle,' he sighed. The bottom sandwich was cheese and pickle too. His face fell further.

'Why don't you get your wife to give you something else for a change?' asked the trainee gently.

'I don't have a wife,' spluttered the salesman. 'I have to make these myself every morning.'

A female sales representative was travelling home one night after an evening spent with the area sales manager. On her way down the motorway she was stopped by a police patrol and breathalysed. She blew into the machine and it immediately changed colour.

'Oh dear,' said the policeman. 'You've had a stiff one tonight.'

'Good grief!' exclaimed the girl, looking embarrassed. 'Does that show too?'

A travelling salesman raced breathlessly onto a station platform in Northern Ireland.

'When is the next train to Belfast?' he asked the porter.

'Sorry, sir,' came the reply. 'The next train has just left.'

A salesman raced into a country pub one evening and asked the landlord, 'Does anyone in this village have a large black dog that wears a white collar?'

'I don't think so,' said the landlord, scratching his head. 'Does anyone here have a black dog with a white collar?' The occupants of the bar all shook their heads.

'Oh my God!' cried the salesman. 'I'm sorry, then, but I've just run over your vicar.'

A company rep was stopped the other day for drinking and driving. The police officer went up to him and asked him to blow into the balloon. 'Certainly, sir,' said the salesman. 'Who's playing in goal?'

A salesman was stopped by a policeman one dark November night. 'Are you aware you have no rear light showing, sir?'

The salesman leapt out of the car and dashed round to the back, where he began to hold his head and mutter distractedly.

'Don't worry, sir, it's not all that serious,' the policeman said sympathetically.

'What do you mean, not serious?' cried the salesman. 'When I set off I had an exhibition caravan on that towbar.'

A salesman was up in court for disorderly behaviour. One of his colleagues was, in his defence, explaining that he and the accused had called in at a pub on the way home to 'steady' themselves after receiving a rocket from their boss.

'You don't think you both had too much to drink?' asked the magistrate.

'Oh no. The only problem was that we both ended up so steady we couldn't move.'

A salesman was travelling in a railway compartment with an American who engaged him in conversation. 'In the States we can board a train in the morning and travel all day and still not reach our destination before nightfall,' he boasted.

The Englishman smiled. 'We have those over here too.'

In the 1930s commercial travellers were held in some esteem. They wore bowler hats and travelled around the country by train. A rather pompous member of the species arrived in a northern town and, gazing condescendingly on the railway porter asked, 'What's the situation in this town regarding hotels?'

The porter sniffed and looked the salesman up and down before saying, 'I don't think you'll have too much trouble getting a job.'

The salesman was up in court for having defrauded his employer out of several thousand pounds — a crime which had led to the bankruptcy of the business and the ruin of his employer.

'How on earth could you have cheated a man who trusted you?' asked the judge despairingly.

'Because it doesn't work with people who don't trust you, your worship,' came the reply.

A salesman developed a fault in his new rear-engined car while out on his calls. As he stood by the side of the road an identical car pulled up to offer assistance.

'What's wrong?' asked his would-be rescuer.

'I don't know,' sighed the salesman, lifting the bonnet, 'but it looks as if my engine's dropped out.'

'You're in luck,' said the other man. 'I don't know about cars either, but I *do* know that there's a spare engine in my boot.'

A salesman had just been presented with his new company car, so he was disappointed to get into it and discover that the engine was dead. After peering under the bonnet for a few moments he decided he needed expert help and called a mechanic. The mechanic took one look and just twiddled a small wire. Immediately the engine started.

'That'll be twelve pounds fifty, please,' he said.

'But that's outrageous!' said the salesman. 'All you did was twiddle a wire.'

'Look,' said the mechanic, 'it's fifty pence for twiddling the wire but it's twelve pounds for knowing which wire to twiddle.'

A sales manager was giving some of his tips to his new door-to-door encyclopaedia salesmen. 'I owe most of my success to the first eight words I uttered whenever a woman opened the door.'

'What were they?' asked an eager young recruit.

'Excuse me, miss, but is your mother in?'

A salesman's car broke down and left him stranded overnight in a remote little town with only one hotel, a sleazy, seedy place. The TV was broken and there was no one in the bar, and he was just wondering what he could do for the evening when, passing an open door, he saw a snooker table and decided to have a solitary game.

The receptionist managed to find him a cue and a set of balls, but everything was so old and grubby that the balls were a uniform grey colour. 'How do you expect me to play with these?' he asked. 'I can't even tell the white from the black.'

'Don't worry,' said the receptionist. 'You'll soon get to know them by their shape.'

A haberdashery salesman was requested to call on an Irish nudist camp. 'What can I do for you?' he asked the manager.

'We need 250 pink ribbons and 250 blue ribbons so that our members can tell who's male and who's female.'

Two young salesmen met up in a sleepy town where there was nothing much going on. They had a few drinks, then one of them leapt to his feet and said, 'I saw a Catholic church up the road, so I'm going to confession.'

'You're crazy,' said the other, but off went his friend.

In the confessional the salesman confessed to the priest that he had made love with a local girl. Naturally concerned, the priest questioned him. Who had it been? The salesman stubbornly refused to say, and although the priest named a number of girls he did not get a satisfactory reply. Eventually the salesman left and returned to his friend in the bar.

'Well,' he asked, 'did you get absolution?'

'No,' said the other man, 'but I got some useful names and addresses. Come on, we're going to have a good evening.'

A salesman called at the office of a major potential customer with the intention of landing a massive sales coup. He handed his card to the great man's secretary and requested a meeting, but when she took it through to her boss he just tore it up and threw it in the bin. Unfortunately for him, the secretary had left the door open a few inches and the salesman saw what happened.

When she returned and told him that her boss would not see him, he politely requested whether he might have his card back. A minute later she emerged from the office with a pound note which she offered to the salesman with an apology. He took it, then pulled out another card. 'The cards are fifty pence each,' he explained, 'so here's another for your boss to keep.'

The great man was so taken by his cheek that he agreed to meet him.

The salesman knew that his company car was getting old and scruffy, but he only realised *how* old when he had a puncture as he was heading up the A1. Pulling onto the hard shoulder, he got out the jack and the spanner and proceeded to take off the wheel. As he was rolling the spare round, he discovered another man with the bonnet up, just about to disconnect the battery.

'What do you think you're doing?' he asked indignantly.

'Look, mate,' the man replied, 'if you're going to have the tyres I'm going to have the bloody battery.'

A salesman found himself marooned in the Orkneys by bad weather and contacted his HQ in Aberdeen with the news. Back came the reply. 'No problem. Take a week's holiday as from yesterday.'

The sales manager was accompanying a nervous newcomer on a tour of the latter's new territory. Unfortunately they experienced some car trouble and they ran out of petrol at the bottom of a steep hill. 'You'll have to walk a mile up the hill to get some petrol,' said the manager. 'Damn it, this is going to hold us up for ages.'

'Why don't I push the car up the hill?' volunteered the salesman, trying to seem eager. The manager agreed, and so the new man pushed the heavy car all the way up the steep hill and to the nearest garage, which was about a mile away. As they pulled into the forecourt the manager wound down his window and looked out at the sweating and gasping salesman.

'Do you smoke?' he asked.

'Yes, I do,' said the salesman, anticipating a large cigar at the very least.

'I'm not surprised,' said the manager. 'You seem to be in a very poor state of fitness.'

Two salesmen were travelling together, the older introducing the younger to his patch, when they had trouble with their car and had to stay for the night at a beautiful manor house. The place was owned by a very attractive mature lady who, they discovered, had been widowed and left with this amazing house and estate.

She was very kind and showed each of them to their rooms where they spent a comfortable night. In the morning they said goodbye and went on their way. More than a year later the two men met at a sales conference.

'Tell me,' said the younger man, 'when we spent that night at the manor, did you by any chance sneak into that lady's bedroom?'

'I did,' admitted the older man.

'And did you use *my* name?'

'I did — you see you're unmarried, and I didn't want my wife getting to hear about it . . .'

'I've just heard from her solicitor,' said the young man.

'This is terrible!' cried the other.

'Not at all. She died last month and left me the house and the estate in her will.'

A group of businessmen were up late one night at their conference hotel discussing a new promotional idea. About midnight they began to feel hungry, so they asked room service to send up some sandwiches. These duly arrived, but they were rather dainty and they didn't last long. The sales manager phoned down again and requested more.

'Just how many do you want?'

The manager counted his colleagues, then picked up the bill. 'Judging from what we got last time for our money, I'd say about sixty pounds' worth.'

The new salesman was attending the company dance and spotted his boss, the sales director, across the room. Turning to a pretty girl next to him, he said, 'Look at the mean old devil. He's the most awful man I've ever met.'

'Is he really?' replied the girl. 'I'll have you know that I'm his daughter.'

The salesman blanched. 'Do you know who *I* am?' he asked.

She shook her head. 'Well thank God for that,' he said.

A young salesman was hauled up before the managing director, who had received complaints about his mounting debts. 'What do you *do* with your salary?' he demanded.

The salesman shrugged. 'Some goes on drink, some on women, some on the horses. The rest I squander.'

A multi-national company booked an entire hotel for its sales conference. On the second day one of the delegates died and the hotel manager sent the undertakers to remove the body. 'It's in room 301,' he told them.

Half an hour later the undertaker called into the manager's office to confirm that the job had been done and the occupant of room 103 had been taken away.

'You idiot!' cried the manager. 'I said room 301. Was the man in 103 dead too?'

'He said he wasn't,' shrugged the undertaker, 'but we all know what terrible liars these salesmen are.'

Two salesmen were discussing the shorthand typist who worked for them both. 'I took her out the other night,' said one, 'and we went back to her place. I've got to tell you, she's terrific in bed, much better than my wife. Why don't *you* take her out? I know she fancies you.'

The other salesman duly did this and reported back to his friend the next day. 'She's certainly good in bed,' he agreed, 'but I wouldn't say she's any better than your wife.'

The son of a company chairman was placed in the sales office in order to learn the business of selling. The office manager was concerned that there should be no ill-feeling among the staff due to the young man's relationship with the owner of the firm. He asked if he might speak to the Chairman on the matter.

'Don't worry,' said the top man. 'I want you just to

treat him as you would anyone else who was to take over the company in the future.'

The Sales Director and his wife were at the company Christmas party, and he was making liberal use of the free bar. 'That's the tenth time you've been to the bar this evening,' his wife wailed. 'What on earth will people think?'

'It's all right,' he told her. 'Every time I get a drink I say it's for you.'

The company dance was in full swing and a very small and young-looking salesman who had had rather a lot to drink went up to the chairman's wife and asked her to dance with him. She gazed down at him disapprovingly and said, 'I would never dance with a child.'

'I'm sorry, I wasn't aware of your condition,' said the salesman.

The Sales Manager called a meeting of all his male staff. 'Have any of you been sleeping with my secretary?' he demanded. His secretary being a stunningly attractive girl who was fairly free with her favours, there were a lot of embarrassed glances and stifled coughs.

'All right, let's try it another way,' he said. 'Is there anyone here who *hasn't* slept with my secretary?' More embarrassed looks. Then one of the salesmen raised his hand.

'I haven't,' he confessed.

'Right,' said the sales manager. '*You're* going to fire her.'

A sales director with a reputation for toughness sent for one of his sales force, a young man who had failed to secure a large order. 'This is the second time you've failed to make an easy sale,' he lectured. 'I should have no hesitation in firing you right now. However, I'm a sporting man and I'm willing to give you a chance to redeem yourself. One of my eyes is a false one. If you can tell which it is I'll allow you to remain on the staff.'

Taking a long look into the sales director's eyes, the young man said, 'The right one is false.'

'You're right. How did you guess?'

'It has a more sympathetic look than the other one.'

The sales manager was giving a dressing-down to one of his young computer salesmen, and he got carried away with himself.

'Don't talk to me like that!' protested the young man. 'I take orders from no one.'

'*Precisely.*'

At a sales conference a famous salesman had been invited to talk about his success. 'I'm sure we can all learn from him,' said the speaker who introduced him. 'For example, he sold two million books in Africa, a continent not normally thought of as a major book market. May we ask you how you did it?'

'That's easy,' said the salesman. 'I sold them as aids to family planning.'

A surprised gasp travelled around the audience. 'Perhaps you'd explain,' said the chairman.

'All I told them was that to prevent pregnancy they just had to take the book and grip it firmly between the knees . . .'

Everyone knew that the sales manager liked a few drinks, but they were all pretty stunned when his wife phoned the office one morning to say that he wouldn't be coming in to work for a month or two.

'He's gone to Canada,' she explained.

'Family troubles?' enquired his deputy.

'No. He saw a notice saying DRINK CANADA DRY, so he thought he'd have a go.'

The sales manager walked into his office and discovered one of his sales reps and his secretary making passionate love on his desk. 'Jenkins!' he screeched. 'Miss Peabody!

What do you think you're doing? And keep still while I'm talking to you.'

In many ways a company is like an orchestra. The string section is like the sales force, fiddling their overtime, expenses and lunches. The Managing Director is the euphonium pumping away in the background all the time. The wind section are the shop stewards. The percussion section is the typing pool, constantly banging away, and the conductor is the chairman, trying to make them all pull together and forever glancing over his shoulder to see the reaction from customers.

'Could I speak to your boss, please?' a man asked the dumb secretary.

'Are you a salesman, a creditor or a friend of his?' she asked.

'I suppose you could say I'm all three,' he smiled.

'Oh.' She thought hard. 'In that case, I'm afraid he's in a meeting. He's away on business. Would you like to come this way?'

What's the difference between an overseas sales director and a wealthy yacht owner and his girlfriend? One is abroad with sales, the other is sailing abroad.

The area manager sat looking through the sales figures for the previous month. Steam seeped from his ears as he noted that one salesman had, yet again, sold less than half that of anyone else on the team.

'That's it, Robinson,' he yelled. 'You're fired!'

'Surely not, sir,' Robinson replied equably. 'Slaves are *sold*, not fired.'

A certain salesman's performance seemed to be suffering and he'd been involved with a number of incidents which had caused complaints from customers, so the company sent him off to see a psychiatrist. 'Tell me about your early life,' said the psychiatrist, so the salesman did, at some length.

After an hour the psychiatrist interrupted. 'There doesn't seem to be anything out of the ordinary in your background. In fact I'll be honest with you and say that you seem as normal and sane as I am.'

'But doctor,' said the salesman, 'what about all these little bugs crawling over my skin? I can't bear them!'

'Aaah!' shrieked the psychiatrist. 'Don't start flicking them all over me!'

A disgruntled salesman overheard one of his bosses mention that he and his family were going on holiday to Wales. 'Wales is good for only two things, prostitutes and rugby,' he muttered as he walked past.

'What was that?' said the boss. 'I'll have you know that my wife was born and bred in Wales.'

The salesman did some quick thinking. 'Really? And what position did she play?'

The marketing manager at a big company became increasingly worried as his colleagues dropped dead around him. First it was his chief salesman, then the overseas buyer, followed in quick succession by the chief executive and the finance director. Stress and good living all seemed to be taking their toll, so he tried to regulate his work and his drinking habits.

One evening he took a rather timid young salesman to the local pub to try and talk a bit of confidence into the boy over a large glass of orange juice. Instead of opening up, the young man just seemed to become more and more subdued. Suddenly the manager became agitated. 'My God, I'm paralysed!' he cried. 'It's my turn next. I'm going to die!'

'What's wrong?' asked the salesman.

'I've been pinching my leg while we've been talking and I can't feel a thing.'

'Thank goodness for that,' blushed the young man. 'It's my leg you've been pinching.'

A British salesman who had been working in a tiny African state got into a bit of local bother and needed to leave the country in a hurry. Unfortunately he couldn't get out over the borders, so he turned for help to a man who was trapping wild animals for export to an English wildlife park.

'Just slip into this gorilla suit,' said the trapper, 'and we'll slip you out in a crate in a day or two.' The salesman did so, and was put in a cage like the other animals. During the night, however, he heard a noise and found that a lion from the cage next door had slipped in with him. As it approached he began to scream with fright.

'Just shut up,' said the lion. 'Anyone would think you were the only person trying to get out of the country.'

The sales director had a new secretary who, though she had seemed very impressive at the interview, was now making awful mistakes in his letters. One day, after he'd given her back another batch for retyping, he snapped, 'I can't think what's wrong. Don't you know the Queen's English?'

'Of course I do,' she protested. 'If she wasn't, she wouldn't be our queen, would she?'

Four salesmen from the same company were sitting together during a lunch break at a conference. As the wine flowed they began to admit their weaknesses.

'I'm fond of the odd bet,' said the most senior. 'Don't tell the boss, but I sometimes put the money I collect for goods on the horses. So far I've won every time, but I know that sooner or later I'll lose the lot.'

'My problem's booze,' said his assistant. 'I've had a few close shaves recently. I live in fear of being banned from driving.'

'It's women that are my little weakness,' said the third. 'In fact I think I've got the boss's daughter pregnant.'

There was a long silence. The three of them turned to the trainee who was sitting silently. 'You must have a fault,' they said. 'What is it?'

'I suppose,' he said, 'that my great weakness is my over-ambition. But,' he smiled, 'I've got a funny feeling that I'm on my way to the top.'

For many years the assistant sales manager was fond of nipping out for a couple of whiskies each lunchtime. To hide the fact from his boss, he always sucked a strong peppermint on his way back to work. One day, in a tearing hurry to get back to his desk, he found he'd run out of mints, so he had a pickled onion instead.

Later, as he leaned across the manager's desk with the latest figures, his boss asked. 'How long have you been working with me?'

'Five years,' said the assistant, surprised.

'That's right,' agreed the manager. 'For five years I've put up with the smell of whisky and peppermints every afternoon. But I warn you, if it's going to be whisky and pickled onions from now on, you're fired!'

The salesman went to his doctor complaining that he was having difficulty sleeping.

'Are you sleeping at night?' asked the doctor.

'Yes,' said the salesman. 'And I'm not having too much trouble nodding off in the mornings. It's just the afternoons that are a bit of a problem.'

The puzzled salesman was talking to a man who ran a local newspaper in a small country town. 'I don't understand how you sell it,' he said. 'After all, in a place as small as this everyone knows what everyone else is doing.'

The newspaper man just smiled. 'They may know what everyone else is doing, but they have to read the paper to find out who's been caught doing it.'

The estate agent was showing a young couple around a house. 'There's something very special about this property,' he told them. 'To the north is the sewage works, to the south the brewery, to the east the gasworks and to the west the abattoir.'

'That isn't special,' cried the woman. 'It's awful!'

'Yes it is special,' said the estate agent. 'It's the only house in the area where you can always tell which way the wind's blowing.'

The salesman took his small son to the zoo. 'Well,' said his mother when they arrived home, 'did you like the zoo?'

'Oh yes,' said the boy. 'And Daddy did too, especially when one of the animals come home at a hundred to one.'

The salesman, letter in hand, entered the office of his secretary, who happened to be very pregnant. 'I think we have a typist's error, here,' he said.

She blushed slightly and patted her tummy. 'Well I won't tell anyone if you don't!'

The sales manager called his team into his office. 'I've got good and bad news for you,' he announced. 'The bad news is that they've cut our commission by three per cent. The good news is that I've persuaded them to backdate it for six months.'

A salesman who had been invited to attend a conference at his company's northern HQ decided to travel by train so that he would be fresh when he arrived first thing in the morning. His secretary duly booked him a sleeper, but he was warned that he would have to share a compartment with another passenger.

He boarded the train on the night and found himself sharing with a middle-aged woman who made eyes at him. Ignoring her, he went to bed, only to be woken in the early hours of the morning by a persistent tapping on the bottom of his bunk. 'Are you awake?' she asked.

'Yes,' he muttered.

'I'm awfully cold,' she said. 'Could you let me have a spare blanket?'

'I've got a better idea,' replied the salesman. 'Let's pretend we're married.'

'There's nothing I'd like more,' she giggled.

'Right,' said the salesman. 'Get your own bloody blanket.'

A salesman was trying to sell a housewife a freezer. 'It'll pay for itself,' he told her. 'You'll save so much on your food bills that you'll soon be making money on it.'

'I appreciate that,' she agreed. 'It's just that at the moment we're paying for our car on the fares we're saving, and our mortgage on the rent we're saving. We honestly can't afford to save any more.'

The young mother was looking at a very sophisticated toy that had been recommended by the salesman for her little boy. 'Isn't it a bit complicated for him?' she asked.

'In fact it's a very educational toy,' said the salesman, 'guaranteed to prepare the child for coping in the modern world. You see, whichever way he puts it together is bound to be wrong.'

In the fabric department of a large store a customer asked one of the sales girls to cut her a metre of material. This the girl did, and asked the customer for three pounds. She also pointed out that, if the customer was interested, there was now a remnant of one and a half metres which she could have for two pounds fifty pence.

'Keep the metre you've just cut,' said the customer. 'I'll take the remnant.'

A newsagent had a shop next door to a bank. One day one of his customers came in and asked him if he could lend him ten pounds, just till the end of the month.

'I'd like to, honestly,' said the newsagent, 'but I've come to an arrangement with the bank. They've promised not to sell cigarettes and newspapers and I've promised not to lend any money.'

A young shopkeeper was explaining business ethics to his girlfriend. 'It's like this,' he said. 'If a customer comes into the shop, buys something that costs ten pounds and gives me a ten pound note which I later discover is *two* ten pound notes stuck together, should I tell my partner?'

A woman raced into a butcher's shop late on Christmas Eve. 'I need a large turkey,' she panted. The butcher had only one bird left, which he was anxious to be rid of, but when he showed it to her she asked for a bigger one.

'I'll just check the cold store,' he said, and disappeared behind the scenes where he wrapped the bird in plastic and put it in a box, which made it look bigger. 'Is this any good?' he asked, emerging again.

'That's fine,' said his customer. Then she paused. 'Look, just to be on the safe side, I'd better take both.'

A lady asked her fishmonger the price of his cod fillets. 'One pound twenty pence a pound,' he told her.

'But it's only one pound a pound down the road,' she exclaimed.

'You'd do better to buy it there, then,' said the fishmonger.

'Oh, they're out of cod,' his customer replied.

'That explains it,' the fishmonger said. 'When I'm out of it *I* sell it for eighty pence a pound.'

Did you hear about the Irish salesman? When he was trained he was taught that personal grooming and cleanliness were very important if he was to impress his clients, so he had clean socks and underwear every day. By Friday he couldn't fasten his trousers or get his shoes on.

A salesman who worked in a gents' outfitters went to confession and told the priest that he had stolen a roll of cloth from the shop.

'I hope you're not going to make a habit of this,' said the priest.

'Actually,' said the salesman, 'I was going to have a jacket made.'

A young man who went on a course,
To learn all about the sales force,
Gave too much concentration
To client penetration,
Now his wife is seeking a divorce.

A brain salesman had called at the house of a man who was going to have a brain transplant. 'I've got two for you to choose from,' he said. 'This one is a teacher's, and it costs £1,000. And this is a politician's, which will cost you £10,000.'

The potential buyer thought a bit. 'Does that mean the politician's brain is better than the teacher's?'

'No,' the salesman shrugged. 'It's just that the politician's is unused.'

The wife of the chief salesman of a major international company was invited to launch a ship that had been built for the company. She was delighted to oblige, but not so happy when she saw an account of the occasion in the company's internal newspaper. It read: 'Mrs Brown smashed a bottle of champagne against her side and then slowly her enormous bulk slid down the slipway to tumultuous cheers from the watching crowd.'

The dictator of a small African country that was experiencing civil unrest arrived unexpectedly at a company manufacturing tanks and armaments somewhere in the Midlands. 'I'm looking for something that will help me to keep my workers in line,' he told the sales manager.

Together they toured the factory looking at the various products, and while they were doing this a hooter sounded and the workforce all leapt up and dashed out. 'Insurrection! Revolution!' cried the visitor. 'This is what they do in *my* country. But look, we can use your tanks to round them up and bring them all back . . .'

'No, no, you don't understand,' interrupted the sales manager. 'In an hour the hooter will sound again and they'll all come back.'

'Well in that case,' said the statesman, 'I'll take five hundred hooters.'

A sales manager received a request for a reference from a company which was considering employing a salesman whom he had fired for laziness. He considered the problem for a long time before writing, 'Dear Sir, If you can get Martin Jones to work for you you will indeed be fortunate ...'

At the end of a long day the buyer of a major retail chain at last had a few moments free and agreed to see a salesman. 'You're very lucky,' he commented as the man entered. 'I've been so busy I've had to refuse to see a dozen reps today.'

'I know,' said the salesman. 'I'm them.'

Some people are born salesmen. Take the Jew who was travelling on a train with a stranger. The stranger guessed his companion's religion and asked him why the Jews were considered such brainy people. 'It's fishcakes that give us our brains,' came the reply, and to prove the fact the Jew took out his lunch of fishcakes.

'In that case, if you've got a fishcake to spare, I'd like to purchase it from you,' said the man.

'Yes, I've got one spare. It will be a pound,' said the Jew, and the man paid up.

'Delicious,' he exclaimed, tucking in. Suddenly he paused. 'You sold me a fishcake for the price of a packet of fish and chips,' he murmured.

'You see,' said his companion. 'It's beginning to work already.'

The sales force of a local company had a very boozy Christmas lunch party the other year, and one of their number ended up being sick down his trousers. Rather than risk a lecture from his wife, on his way to the station he popped into a discount clothing store. 'A pair of trousers,' he said. 'Thirty-six inch waist and plain grey in colour.' The assistant stuffed the trousers into a paper bag and handed them to him. He managed to find an empty compartment on the train home, and as it pulled out of the station he removed his smelly old trousers. Not knowing where to put them, he rolled them up and threw them out of the window. Then he opened the paper bag — and found that he'd bought a red nylon polo-necked sweater . . .

Did you hear about the salesman who had three successive jobs? He started out selling elastic but was sacked for being too tight. Then he travelled in ladies' underwear, but was arrested for indecency. Eventually he ended up selling All Bran because he liked the regular hours.

An insurance salesman was approached by a man of ninety-seven who wished to take out a life insurance policy. The old chap filled out a form and had a medical, despite all attempts to put him off, but eventually his application was turned down.

'I'm afraid the risks are just too great,' the insurance man told him.

'You're mad,' protested the old boy. 'Just check the mortality figures and you'll find that very few men die over the age of ninety-seven.'

During a long sales conference an invited speaker gave a long and dreary speech at a mid-week dinner. Unfortunately he droned on and on and showed no signs of stopping. There was a lot of coughing and shuffling of feet, but still he didn't stop. One young employee, who had had far too much to drink, was spotted creeping up behind the speaker with a port decanter, apparently intending to hit him on the head with it. Unfortunately he missed his target and instead hit the head of the guest alongside him. As he slumped forward in a daze, the man was heard to beg, 'Hit me again, I can still hear him.'

A sales manager who had often used a certain hotel when he had been a salesman in the area, took his new bride there for their honeymoon. On their first morning he and his new wife came down to the dining-room for breakfast.

'Where's my honey?' the salesman asked the waiter when he brought the toast. The waiter cast an embarrassed glance at the blushing new wife and whispered, as quietly as he could, 'I'm afraid she doesn't work here any more, sir.'

A salesman used to pass his son's school on the way to work in the mornings, so he always dropped the child off. One day he had some paperwork to complete before he went to the office, so his wife took the little boy to school instead. That evening the salesman asked his son if he had enjoyed the novelty of being driven to school by his mother.

'Oh yes, and we didn't see a single silly bastard on the whole journey,' replied his son.

A salesman who had been feeling unwell went to see his doctor and had an extensive check-up. The doctor seemed very subdued. 'Would you like the good news or the bad news first?' the doctor asked.

'The good news,' said the salesman.

'The good news is that by the time you receive my bill you'll be dead.'

A salesman who was a keen golfer decided he would pay for a lesson from the club professional in an attempt to iron out his problems. Having watched his pupil's swing several times, the pro said, 'Why not play golf like you behave at work?'

'What do you mean?' asked the man.

'Well, I'm told by your colleagues that you always take

every opportunity to get your head down and keep it there.'

The estate agent was checking his little son's homework.

'Daddy, what's six times four?' the boy asked.

'Are you buying or selling?' his father replied.

A group of immigrants landed in Australia in the early part of this century. The party contained three men who had been salesmen in their home lands. One was American, one German and one English. Ten years passed and the American owned three hotels, the German had three factories and the Englishman was still waiting to be introduced.

The sales manager of a large company arrived in a small town to attend a dinner at which he was to be principal speaker. Since he was to make a speech the following day to the Chamber of Commerce in the town he asked the local newspaper reporter not to print any of his jokes. The speech went well, but the reporter must have felt disgruntled, because when an account of the occasion appeared it read, 'the principal speaker told several stories which we were unable to print.'

The sales manager had been out with his wife at a company dance and on the way home he was stopped by the police for reckless driving. Instead of cooperating he was awkward and belligerent and refused to get out of the car to be breathalysed. 'I'm awfully sorry, officer,' said his poor wife, trying to defuse the situation. 'He always gets like this when he's drunk.'

On his way home from work a salesman bought some flowers for his wife as a surprise. As she opened the door to greet him he handed her the bouquet — and she immediately burst into tears. 'Whatever is the matter?' the husband asked.

His wife sobbed. 'I've had a terrible day. The washing-machine leaked on the floor, the cat got run over, the freezer's defrosted, and now here you are, *drunk*!'

A speaker at a sales dinner droned on interminably and when he eventually sat down there was a great surge of relief all round. One of the diners, noted for his optimism, said to his neighbour, 'Never mind, there's a good side to everything. After that the winter won't seem so long.'

The managing director of a large company owned a race-horse and used to invite his staff to watch it run. One day he took his sales director with him to Newmarket. In the saddling enclosure he stood and watched the trainer helping the jockey saddle up. The sales director noticed the trainer give the horse something to eat.

'What's that?' he asked curiously.

'Just a sweet, sir,' replied the trainer. 'Would you like one?' The sales director accepted the offer.

As he gave the jockey a leg-up the trainer murmured quietly 'Hold him back for the first six furlongs, then let him go. If anything passes you in the final quarter mile it'll be the sales director.'

A group of salesmen who had been urged to get fit by their boss were in the habit of working out and having a sauna at the end of the day. Several of them were sitting naked in the sauna one evening when two ladies opened the door and, not realising their mistake, stepped inside the cabin. All of the salesmen grabbed their towels and wrapped them around themselves except one, who covered his head.

When the embarrassed ladies had gone, the other salesmen demanded an explanation of his strange behaviour. 'I don't know about you lot,' he said, 'but around here I'm known by my face . . .'

One evening a good-looking young salesman was driving to Birmingham in a company van packed with exhibition equipment and goods. A few miles from home he picked up a stunningly beautiful girl who was hitch-hiking, and after a few minutes conversation and meaningful glances he pulled off the main road and parked on a quiet grass verge.

The front of the van being very cramped, there wasn't much room for manoeuvre, so they climbed out, intending to make love on the grass. Unfortunately it was raining, so they crawled under the van. They were hard at it when the salesman looked up to find a policeman looming over him.

'What do you think you're doing?' asked the policeman.

'I'm mending my van,' replied the salesman quickly.

'No, you're not,' said the constable. 'I'll give you three reasons why. First, you're the wrong way up. Second, a small crowd that has just turned out of the pub is cheering you on. And third, someone's nicked your van.'

Everyone tried to be polite about the launch of the new product, but things didn't go very well. In fact, according to one of the people present, 'The product was as useless as the sales manager, the sales manager was as wet as the tea, the tea was as tasteless as the chairman's wife, the chairman's wife was as old as the office furniture, the office furniture as stylish as the toilet seat, the toilet seat as clean as the manager's collar, the manager's collar as tight as the designer, the designer as attractive as his product, the product was as useless . . .'

The shoe-shop manager had had several pairs of a certain brand of shoe returned with complaints that it fell apart after a few months' wear. 'We'll cover ourselves by putting up a sign,' he told his staff. And he produced a notice, which he placed in the window by the shoes, reading: THIS SHOE IS FIT FOR A QUEEN.

'But it's one of the worst-made shoes we stock!' gasped an assistant.

'And just how much walking does a queen have to do?'

Yorkshire cricket lovers raced to the paper kiosk, where the paper seller was yelling 'Yorkshire do it again! Read all about it!' On close inspection one customer discovered that Yorkshire's score was a measly 53 for 7. Having expected more successful news he asked the paper-seller to explain his sales pitch.

'Well it's the fifth disaster they've had,' said the seller, quite unabashed.

Sales Stories

Every salesman knows that real life is far funnier than any joke — so here's a selection of true anecdotes and stories covering all aspects of the sales force, from retailing to advertising.

A travelling salesman brought up for speeding in Lechlade, Gloucestershire in 1974 told the court, 'I forgot myself. But at the far end of town they were screaming for toilet rolls.'

Salesmen beware! A Dutch computer firm recently displayed its wares at a British exhibition. Fifteen-year-old Simon Kaye took a look at their product and proceeded to suggest ways of making it cheaper and more competitive.

The salesmen took notes and sent them to head office, who confirmed that young Simon's advice was correct. As a thankyou they offered him a free computer but he declined, saying that he already had seven.

A thirty-two-year-old carpet salesman from Maryland, USA, was told by his doctor that he was suffering from Crohn's disease and had only three months to live. Deciding to make the most of it, the man embezzled $30,000 from the company and went on a spending spree, drinking, dining and generally enjoying himself. Only one thing bothered him, and that was the fact that his health didn't seem to be deteriorating. In fact, as the weeks passed, he was beginning to feel better.

Worried, he sought a second opinion — and it was revealed that, far from suffering Crohn's disease, he had a simple hernia and an allergy problem.

A German campaign to boost sales of washing-powder quoted a housewife as saying, 'I wouldn't swap one packet of my favourite powder for two of any other make.'

The company was inundated with letters from housewives saying that *they* certainly would accept the deal, and one man even tried to swap a ton of their product for two tons of a rival brand.

Asked to comment on the fact that sales of mistletoe were falling, a salesman said, 'It's a fast disappearing thing now people have sex all the year round.'

Questioned about the presence of a black girl clad in a feather boa on his stand at the Motor Show, the then Sales Director of the Lotus sports car company said, 'You have to understand what our car is all about. I won't say that the man who buys one of our yellow dropheads is running a mistress, but he wants to make his friends wonder if he is running one. A coloured girl is the great status symbol in mistresses at the moment. It's a subliminal message we're putting across.'

A South Humberside man who was applying for a job described his present post as 'transport manager' at a supermarket. He was in fact in charge of the trolleys in the shop.

Always think before you speak. Brian Johnston, the cricket commentator, didn't. Which was why, during a Test Match between England and the West Indies he uttered the line 'The bowler's Holding, the batsman's Willey.'

In the heyday of Hollywood one salesman found himself with a sales pitch that covered some of the most remote parts of South America. Arriving in a small town in Venezuela he went to the local cinema owner and offered him the latest Clark Gable picture.

'But Clark Gable is dead,' said the man.

'No, he's not,' said the salesman.

'Yes he is,' insisted the cinema proprietor. 'Didn't you see his last film?'

'Yes,' said the salesman.

'He died in it. If you saw it, you must know.'

'But it was only a film, he was acting!' protested the salesman.

'Can't a man believe the evidence of his own eyes?' responded the cinema owner. 'We saw him die. There would be a riot if we showed another Clark Gable picture.'

In 1948 British and American car manufacturers visited the Volkswagen plant to take a look at the Beetle. 'The Volkswagen,' they decided, 'does not meet the fundamental technical requirements of a motor car.'

They went on to invest $350 million in a new car, the Edsel — which went out of production, one of the worst failures in manufacturing history, only two years later.

In 1897 the Remington Company turned down the offer of a patent writing machine, an early typewriter, with the words, 'no mere machine can replace a reliable and honest clerk.'

A London amusement arcade manager went all the way to Paris in 1970 to investigate a new and very expensive fortune-telling computer. When he tried it out, the machine produced for him a lengthy prediction which included the warning, 'If you are contemplating signing any contracts today, do not.'

He chose to ignore the advice and bought the computer. It was a mistake. Five weeks later, having cost him thousands and brought him little custom, it was returned to the manufacturer.

The council of a Canadian town was having difficulty in selling its cemetery plots, so a resolution was passed cancelling a previous regulation which said that people had to be dead before they could purchase a plot. 'That could explain why they're not selling too well,' commented the mayor.

Sometimes a company is so concerned with producing and selling its product that it ignores problems close to home. Take, for example, the wood preservative firm, Cuprinol Ltd, which was disturbed to find that while its products were preserving thousands of homes, the floor of its company canteen was riddled with wet rot . . .

Alfred Bloomingdale, owner of the world-famous department store, once produced a musical which opened in Boston before moving to Broadway. The critics didn't like it, and when Bloomingdale asked George S. Kaufman for his advice he told him, 'If I were you, I'd close the show and keep the store open at night.'

Mr Arthur Cox, who owns a shop, hates VAT so much that he refuses to stock anything that carries VAT. So he sells ordinary biscuits but not chocolate ones, and canned fish but not cat food. However, he has to be registered for VAT so that he can claim back VAT-rated items such as paper bags that have to be used in the shop. This means that the VAT man has to pay him, but he doesn't have to pay a penny.

A Nottingham travel agent was interviewed by the local paper on the problems of selling holidays in Belfast. He insisted that the troubles were having little effect on his trade. 'It's going on every day in Belfast. I don't think bombs have the same sort of "feel" about them that they might have done some years ago.'

In Moscow in 1983 a brand new ophthalmic centre, packed with all the latest technology and diagnostic measures to advise on people's sight problems was opened. Unfortunately its opening coincided with a national shortage of spectacle frames and lenses, though more were promised in a year or two.

An elderly Chicago lady got lost one day in one of the city's huge department stores. She claimed that, unable to find her way out, she spent a month living in the shop until she was eventually found in the bedding department. She had opened an account and lived off the things she bought, even eating in the restaurant!

A dress manufacturer was faced with an angry customer who had only discovered *after* she had got her new dress home that it could be neither dry-cleaned nor washed.

His reply was dismissive. 'I don't expect my clothes to be worn more than once.'

A nun found leaving an Oxford Street store with two cardigans in her bag was charged with shoplifting. When she appeared in court she explained that her misdemeanour had been 'the work of the devil'.

The vice-president of sales for an American corporation had been on a business trip to St Louis and promised his wife to arrive home on an early evening plane. Unfortunately he missed it, and by the time he managed to call her she had already left for the airport.

Finding her husband wasn't on the plane, she left messages on the answerphones of four of his friends in St Louis, asking if he'd decided to change his plans and was staying the night with them. Then she went home.

A couple of hours later her husband arrived and explained what had happened. But throughout the evening his friends called one by one to assure his wife that he was staying with them . . .

Salesmen are rarely popular. The nineteenth-century poet Thomas Campbell once shocked his fellow guests at a literary dinner by drinking to the health of Napoleon Bonaparte. Cries of horror greeted this action but he turned them to laughter by reminding them that Bonaparte once shot a book salesman.

Always have confidence in your product, that's what the sales force is told. And the team that sold the Thermofax copier did have confidence. What was more they sold thousands of the machines. Everything looked bright. Then came the bad news. After a week or two in the files, Thermofax copies turned black.

You don't just have to have the right product. It has to work, too. In 1983 a Norwegian health club owner 'discovered' a revolutionary new diet that went down a treat with his customers. It included beer and ice cream and was very popular — until members noticed that their waistlines were growing. In protest at his behaviour, they burned down his club.

Have faith in your products. The BBC did when they imported *The Thorn Birds,* an American TV show, in 1984. Every critic who saw it panned it; few programmes have ever received such appalling reviews. Despite that, the people who really count loved it so much that 22 million of them switched on their sets for one episode — and an extra power station had to be brought into operation to cope with the power demand.

One of the first things salesmen have to learn is to keep copies of their documents. Sam Goldwyn believed in keeping copies, too. Someone once asked him if he would allow the disposal of all correspondence files over six years old in order to save space. He gave his permission, but said, 'Make copies first.'

In 1975 Smirnoff launched an advertising campaign for

their vodka. One of their famous adverts showed a dusky lady and the line. 'I thought the Kama Sutra was an Indian restaurant until I discovered Smirnoff.'

Then some market research was done — and it was shown that sixty per cent of those questioned *did* think that the Kama Sutra was an Indian restaurant . . .

Sales promotions and free offers can get horribly complicated, as a Worcester man found when he posted off 2,000 cigarette coupons with a request for a free watch. Before long he received a golf bag, a pressure cooker, a doll, two electric blankets, various records, a number of pots, pans and tape recorders and a number of other items, including a wristwatch.

Being an honest man, he kept the watch and sent back the other stuff. In gratitude the tobacco company sent him 10,000 more coupons. With these he ordered some household tools and a bedspread. Back though the post came a plant stand and two stepladders . . .

Looking for a macho-sounding name for their pork and beans product, which was to be launched on the Canadian market, an advertising agency settled on 'Gros Jos.' Fortunately a French-speaking member of the team was able to stop them in time. The colloquial translation of 'Gros Jos' was 'big tits'.

The Parker Pen Company produced a pen which contained new ink which would not leak and would 'prevent embarrassment' caused by black stains. In the course of the overseas selling promotion the word 'embarrassment' was mis-translated as *embarazar* — which means 'to prevent pregnancy'.

The company was inundated with demands for the new wonder contraceptive and had to make swift changes to their claims for the pen's powers.

A sales campaign for a new soap powder didn't work as well as expected in Saudi Arabia. Executives puzzled over it but simply couldn't understand why. It was a simple enough advert. On the left of the poster was a pile of grubby washing. In the middle a smiling lady was shown bundling the washing into a machine. And on the right was a heap of gleaming white garments. Then some bright spark remembered that the Arabs read from right to left . . .

Advertising can help sales — but sometimes it's more of a hindrance. Take those famous adverts in which the late Leonard Rossiter poured a drink over Joan Collins. They became classics, loved by everyone. But can you remember the name of the product they were promoting? If you can, you're in a minority. Follow-up research showed that viewers loved the adverts so much they didn't take any notice of the drink itself, and so they were scrapped.

Sometimes even bright-sounding ideas don't sell. Like the American newspaper that was set up to publish nothing but good news, its owners thinking that everyone would like to hear something cheerful for a change. Unfortunately headlines like, 19,459,483 CITIZENS WERE NOT KILLED IN AUTO ACCIDENTS THIS YEAR were not what people wanted to know.

Sponsorship can backfire — as it did on Benson and Hedges during their tennis tournament at Wembley. Their star player, John McEnroe, called for a ban on smoking. 'Can't breathe this side of the net,' he protested. 'It's like a London fog.'

The manufacturers of a certain brand of male contraceptive couldn't understand why the small and medium sizes of their product were consistently outsold by the large size. After all, they had done a great deal of careful research and they knew there was a market.

In an attempt to solve the problem, they called in a team of marketeers to find out what was going wrong. After a great deal of time and money spent pondering the problem, the product was relaunched — still in three sizes but this time labelled Large, Super and Giant . . .

Birds Eye's new product, Cod Pieces, had been fully developed by the time someone began to wonder whether the name was well chosen.

In the 1950s the Pepsodent toothpaste company decided to move into South East Asia and began an aggressive advertising campaign promising whiter teeth. Nothing happened, and an investigation discovered the inhabitants of the area enjoyed chewing betel nut, which stains the teeth. Betel nut is expensive, and the richer the locals, the blacker their teeth. No one *wanted* white teeth.

Determined to exploit his brother's popularity as president of the USA, Billy Carter launched 'Billy's Beer' in 1977. Unfortunately he got the timing wrong. Jimmy's career began to sink fast, and so did sales of Billy's beer. And things weren't helped by Miss Lillian, their mother who, far from endorsing the product, told the world, 'I tried it once, but it gave me diarrhoea.'

A manufacturer of a foot deodorant known as Pulvapies decided to cash in during an election in Ecuador and devised an advertising campaign which included slogans such as 'Vote for any candidate. But for well-being and hygiene — vote Pulvapies,' and 'For Mayor — Honourable Pulvapies'.

So impressed were the locals that they duly elected a foot deodorant to be their mayor . . .

Don't believe adverts. You think that's a bit strong? Giovanni Martinelli, a famous Italian opera singer who joined the New York Metropolitan Opera, was asked by a reporter how he managed to smoke and sing so brilliantly.

'I would not think if it!' the singer replied.

The reporter pointed out that Martinelli had asserted in

an advert that a certain brand of cigarettes did not irritate his throat.

'Of course I gave that endorsement,' Martinelli said. 'How could they irritate my throat? I have never smoked!'

One of the biggest flops in advertising history was that for Strand cigarettes. It featured a trench-coated man standing alone in the rain on a street corner and lighting a cigarette to comfort himself. Although it wasn't explicit, it looked as if he had been stood up by his girlfriend — and no one wanted to identify with the kind of man who got stood up!

You sometimes have to adapt a product to ensure that it will sell in your market. Take the case of Radclyffe Hall's book *The Well of Loneliness.* When Sam Goldwyn heard how well it was selling he decided to buy the film rights.

'You won't be able to film the book,' an assistant warned him. 'It's about lesbians.'

'No problem,' Goldwyn replied. 'Where the book's got Lesbians we'll use Austrians.'

Sales Line

Whether you're looking for a provocative quotation on which to base a conference speech, words of wisdom from unexpected sources, or hilarious examples of bad commercial judgement, you'll find something suitable here.

Rolls Royce announced today that it is recalling all Rolls Royce cars made after 1966 because of the faulty nuts behind the wheel.

Walter Cronkite.

I have heard of a man who had in mind to sell his house, and therefore carried a piece of brick in his pocket which he shewed as a pattern to encourage purchasers.

The Irish way of selling, described by Jonathan Swift.

It's not the employer who pays the wages — it's the products.

Henry Ford.

When you are getting kicked from the rear it means you are in front.

Bishop Fulton Sheen.

Naturally enough for a company the size of Beecham, the year brought its problems. The pharmaceutical side of the business, including proprietary medicines, was clearly not helped by the very low level of winter sickness throughout the northern hemisphere.

Annual report of the Beecham Group chairman.

No one has endurance like the man who sells insurance.

Traditional insurance maxim.

It is well known what a middle man is; he is a man who bamboozles one party and plunders the other.

Disraeli.

These eggs aren't all they're cracked up to be.

My tool has given considerable satisfaction.

Our Bristol factory went bust in 1981.

My wife is much happier with the carpet now that she has her underfelt.

Extracts from letters sent to sales departments.

When I sell liquor it's called bootlegging; when my patrons serve it on silver trays on Lake Shore Drive, it's called hospitality.

Al Capone.

It used to be that people needed products to survive. Now products need people to survive.

Nicholas Johnson.

Business is simply other people's money.

Alexander Dumas.

Cars new and pre-owned.

Sign in a car dealer's window.

Nothing is as irritating as the fellow who chats pleasantly to you while he's overcharging you.

Kim Hubbard.

Dear Madam,

With reference to your blue raincoat, our manufacturers have given the garment in question a thorough testing, and find that it is absolutely waterproof. If you will wear it on a dry day and then take it off and examine it, you will see that our statement is correct.

Letter from a rainwear manufacturer to a dissatisfied customer.

The basis of optimism is sheer terror.

Oscar Wilde.

Customers giving orders will be swiftly executed.

Sign in a Hong Kong tailor's shop.

A man without a smile must not open a shop.

Proverb.

Closed until we open.

Sign in a Polish bicycle shop.

Experience is a name everyone gives to their mistakes.

Oscar Wilde.

Experience is a marvellous thing. It enables you to recognise a mistake whenever you make it again.

Saturday Evening Post.

When a man comes to me for advice I find out the kind of advice he wants and I give it to him.

Josh Billings.

He that travels knows much.

Thomas Fuller.

Tact is the ability to describe others as they see themselves.

Abraham Lincoln.

The true concept of business is: do other men for they would do you.

Charles Dickens.

The trouble with being punctual is that nobody's there to appreciate it.

Franklin P. Jones.

If at first you don't succeed, try, try again. Then quit. There's no use being a damn fool about it.

W.C. Fields.

Advertising may be described as the science of arresting the human intelligence long enough to get money from it.

Stephen Leacock.

I do not read advertisements — I would spend all my time wanting things.

Archbishop of Canterbury.

The consumer is not a moron. She is *your* wife. And she is grown up.

David Ogilvy.

We don't think the Beatles will do anything in this market.

Jay Livingstone, Capitol Records.

Next to the American corpse, the American bride is the hottest thing in today's merchandising market.

Kitty Hanson.

Some are born great, some achieve greatness and some hire public relations officers.

Daniel Boorstin.

THE HITE REPORT ON MALE SEXUALITY
£12.50 (cased) £9.95 (limp)

Book advert.

SALES STAFF REQUIRED. NO OBJECTION TO SEX.

Card in employment agency window.

It is our job to make women unhappy with what they have.

B. Earl Puckett.

Public relations is the art of winning friends and getting people under the influence.

Jeremy Tunstall.

You can fool all the people all the time if the advertising is right and the budget is big enough.

Joseph Levine.

There are a million definitions of public relations. I have found it to be the craft of arranging the truth so that people will like you.

Alan Harrington.

A good advert should be like a good sermon; it must comfort the afflicted, it must also afflict the comfortable.

Bernice Fitzgibon.

The philosophy behind much advertising is based on the old observation that every man is really two men — the man he is and the man he wants to be.

William Feather.

An advertising agency; eighty-five per cent confusion and fifteen per cent commission.

Fred Allen.

Doing business without advertising is like winking at a girl in the dark. *You* know what you're doing but no one else does.

Stewart Britt.

If advertising encourages people to live beyond their means, so does matrimony.

Bruce Barton.

Statistics are like a bikini. What they reveal is suggestive but what they conceal is vital.

Aaron Levenstein.

There are too many one ulcer men holding down two ulcer jobs.

Prince Philip.

If the British people liked work as much as they like sport and were as interested in economics as in, say, gardening, we should be at the top of all world tables of industrial nations.

John Hill.

A genius is one who can do anything except make a living.

Joey Adams.

The trouble with the rat race is that even if you win, you're still a rat.

Lily Tomlin.

Work is the curse of the drinking classes.

Oscar Wilde.

The reason why worry kills more people than work is that more people worry than work.

Robert Frost.

My father taught me to work; he did not teach me to love it.

Abraham Lincoln.

I like work. I can sit and look at it for hours. I love to keep it by me; the idea of getting rid of it nearly breaks my heart.

Jerome K. Jerome.

Anyone can do any amount of work provided that it isn't the work he is supposed to be doing at the moment.

Robert Benchley.

I'll give you a definite maybe.

Sam Goldwyn.

You can dismiss from your mind that we are holding back technical developments. As far as we are concerned, there is no consumer demand for a long-life bulb.

Thorn Lighting spokesman.

The two great tragedies of life — not getting what you want and getting it.

Oscar Wilde.

If you are wishful, to do your business with us the movements of our staff will be reserved for your inspection.

The contents of our wine bottles have been individually passed by our manager.

If you should show an interest our representative will be welcome to expose his briefs to you at any moment.

Translated sales brochures sent to English salesmen.

It is a project which, as far as I can see, has a viable marketing opportunity ahead of it.

Giles Shaw, Northern Ireland's Minister of Commerce, on the De Lorean car.

You should make a point of trying every experience once, except incest and folk dancing.

Arnold Bax.

Anything that won't sell, I don't want to invent.

Thomas Edison.

If they're going to get anywhere, it will have to be without the vile-looking singer with the tyre-tread lips.

TV producer after the Rolling Stones' first TV performance.

There's a sucker born every minute.

P.T. Barnum.

A verbal contract isn't worth the paper it's written on.

Sam Goldwyn.

Competition brings out the best in products and the worst in people.

David Sarnoff.

Nothing that costs only a dollar is worth having.

Elizabeth Arden.

Electric light will never take the place of gas.

Werner Von Siemens.

It's a Fact

Which Roman god represents both salesmen and *thieves? Which best-selling board game was turned down for having '52 fundamental errors?' Find out in this selection of strange facts and bizarre sales stories!*

The first woman ever to place a lonely-hearts advert in a British newspaper was a spinster from Manchester called Helen Morrison. Her advert appeared in the *Manchester Weekly Journal* in 1727. When the mayor of Manchester saw it he committed her to a lunatic asylum for a month.

The first coin-operated slot machines for dispensing products were invented by a Greek in the first century AD.

The safety razor was invented and marketed by King C. Gillette. At first it looked as if his development was a dud. When it went on sale in 1903 only 51 razors and 168 blades were sold. Things picked up the following year, though. 90,000 razors and 12,400,000 blades were sold!

It's true, someone *has* sold refrigerators to Eskimos. They use them to prevent food from freezing solid. And the Saudi Arabian government has bought several snow-ploughs — to clear sand off the roads.

The author of a book called *Nutrition for Health* was not a good advert for his ideas. He died of malnutrition.

An American record company had such a success with their release 'The Best of Marcel Marceau' that they are planning a follow-up. Monsieur Marceau is, of course, a mime artist, and the record contains nothing but silences followed by applause.

A British firm once landed an order to export 1,800 tons of sand to Abu Dhabi — one of the most desert-covered countries in the world.

The Scottish distillery of Bruichladdich launched a fifteen-year-old malt whisky in 1982. To make it different from all the others on the market they commissioned special crystal decanters and a lockable Victorian-style tantalus to hold them. The job of the salesmen was to persuade people to part with £1,000 for each of them . . .

The Roman god of merchants and salesmen was Mercury, who was also the god of thieves.

Arthur Ferguson has to be one of the most successful salesmen of all times. In 1923 he sold Big Ben and Nelson's Column to an American couple who paid £1,000 and £6,000 respectively. So smooth-talking was he that he also convinced would-be buyers into parting with a deposit of £2,000 for Buckingham Palace.

When Harrods introduced the very first escalator in Britain, they stationed attendants at the top to administer brandy and smelling salts to any customer who was overcome by the experience.

One of the biggest bargains of all time? In 1626 an anonymous Indian chief sold the island of Manhattan to Governor Peter Minuit for $24 worth of supplies. These days

Manhattan land and real estate prices are among the highest in the world.

It's a fact that extroverts sleep better than introverts. So the more outgoing a salesman, the better he sleeps at night.

You can fool some of the people some of the time ... A physician called Dr Koch made a substantial fortune in the first half of this century with a patent medicine said to cure cancer and TB. When analysed in 1943 it was said to be indistinguishable from distilled water.

Even the sales potential of some of the world's most successful products wasn't at first realised. Take Monopoly, for example. When it was first offered to Parker Brothers in the USA they rejected it, saying that it had '52 fundamental errors'.

They say that there's always room for an improved product in the market. Take mousetraps, for example. An American inventor designed one that was smart and reusable and retailed at only twice the price of the old throwaway variety. Use it to catch two mice and after that you were saving money!

Unfortunately no one bought it. The inventor had overlooked one thing. No one wants to remove a squashed mouse from a trap; they'd rather throw the whole thing away.

'Come alive with Pepsi' was a successful advertising slogan in America, but translated into German its effect wasn't quite the same. 'Rise from the grave with Pepsi' was one translation.

General Motors couldn't understand why their Chevrolet Nova wasn't selling well in Spanish-speaking America. Then someone pointed out that in Spanish 'No va' meant 'won't go'.

A nine-year-old visitor to a museum in County Durham politely pointed out to one of the curators that an exhibit they had labelled as a Roman *sesterce* coin was in fact a plastic token given away in a sales promotion by a soft drinks company.

A woman who fainted at a supermarket check-out in Nuremberg, West Germany, was discovered to have a frozen chicken under her hat — presumably she was attempting to smuggle it out of the store. She ended up in hospital with suspected brain damage.

A Parisian grocer was jailed for two years in 1978 for stabbing his wife to death with a wedge of cheese.

Public relations exercises can cause headaches — and even before PR was invented there were problems. Take the inaugural run of the railway that went from St Louis to Jefferson City in 1955. Two hundred passengers had embarked, and it was only when they failed to arrive at their destination that someone remembered that they hadn't yet connected the track across the bridge over the Gasconade River . . .

Advertisement in a New Zealand paper: OTAGO STUD FARM REQUIRES SINGLE YOUNG MAN.

Anxious to boost the number of passengers on their buses, an East Anglian bus company decided to promote the service with bus bingo. Numbers were displayed on the sides of buses and bingo cards were distributed to people living in the area. When they spotted numbers they just crossed them off their cards.

A car dealer in Coventry bought a twenty foot high fibreglass statue of King Kong as a sales gimmick and then renamed his company the King Kong Car Company. The Department of Trade were not keen on this marketing strategy. They wrote to him forbidding the use of the term King Kong because it implied 'royal patronage.'

When petrol companies first introduced fully automatic petrol pumps, the sort that accept notes and dispense petrol, they tried the idea out in a few selected garages and watched customer reaction.

Few people got the hang of it to begin with. One lady stuffed a pound note down the pump's nozzle and proceeded to shout her order into it. One man wrote his name and address on a piece of paper and inserted it in the slot intended for his one pound note. Asked why, he told observers, 'It said "Insert a note" so I did.'

Bright ideas are invaluable when it comes to selling, but careful research is even more important. Some plucky salesman must have persuaded a Scottish council to buy special protective clothing for its lollipop ladies. In theory it was a great idea — special jerkins that lit up at night to warn drivers. But no one thought to consult the lollipop ladies themselves, and they were none too keen on having their flashing bosoms lit up for all to see.

The Royal Melbourne Golf Club decided to sell off some bushland bordering the course for a building development. Unfortunately the person in charge of the sale got the deeds confused and sold off the eighth, ninth, tenth and eleventh fairways.

Cyril Lord's carpet company thought they'd have a huge success with their British version of 'Astroturf' artificial grass carpeting. Unfortunately the product turned out to have a built-in problem. After a few weeks it turned from green to blue . . .

Advertisement: Fashionable Chiswick Village. Set in attractive communal grounds with trees (tenants have their own small private parts).

Give your customers something that sounds really good. When the stage show of *Grease* went to Mexico it was retitled *Vaseline.* In Paris it was *Brilliantine.* And in Tokyo it was *Glease.*

In China they've found a way to boost the sales of dull books. They package them up with sex manuals, so that along with the facts of life purchasers can also learn the joys of subjects like *How to Repair Electrical Goods.*

Sales Brief

In this section you'll find dozens of brief jokes and wry observations to slip into your speech. They're ideal for breaking the ice quickly when you start and for linking your themes and jokes as you go along. Don't labour these one-liners, just drop them casually into your speech and allow the audience to spot them.

Did you hear about the table linen salesman who signed a contract to supply Barry Manilow with tablecloths to blow his nose on?

One of our salesmen was held up the other week by a man who waved a bunch of flowers at him. It was robbery with violets.

A friend of mine used to be a clock salesman until his company was wound up.

Who wants to be a success anyway? All success involves is making more money to pay the taxes you wouldn't have to pay if you didn't make so much money in the first place.

A friend of mine used to sell bras, but then the company went bust.

There was an advert for gardening services in the local

paper. It read, DON'T KILL YOURSELF IN THE GARDEN, LET US DO IT FOR YOU.

Another advert read, FOR SALE. MANURE £1 A BAG. DO IT YOURSELF 50P.

People do live in the strangest kind of houses. The estate agent had one in his window the other day. COTTAGE, TWO BEDS, it said. SITTING/DINING ROOM, KITCHEN, TOILET 6 MILES FROM BRISTOL.

My friend the bra salesman decided to get out of the business and form a holding company of his own.

Success as a salesman is just a matter of luck — ask any failure.

If you hype something and it sells, you're acclaimed as a genius — it couldn't have been hype. It you hype something and it doesn't sell, then it was just hype.

Did you hear about the head salesman with a firm of dungaree manufacturers? He was congratulated on his overall performance.

There are two ways in which young salesmen thrown in at the deep end survive. One is by crawling and the other is breast stroking.

Every salesman should read the *Sun* — it's the best way of keeping abreast of the market.

Door to door salesmen are like fitted carpets. Everyone walks over them.

Did you hear about the Irish paint salesman who was dismissed from his job for stealing some cans of yellow paint? He was caught red-handed.

Experience is what you get when you fail to get what you really wanted.

FOR SALE: Set of drawers belonging to a lady with bandy legs due to past misuse.

Life as a book salesman has its surprises. Only the other day someone asked for *Tess of the Dormobiles.*

The salesman who can smile when things go wrong has just thought of someone else he can blame it all on.

A proverb for our times. People who live in glass houses are constantly pestered by double-glazing salesmen.

Always remember that no matter how much you sell, you'll never sell enough. And the things you don't sell will be far more important than those you do.

If you can't get a day's work done in twenty-four hours, try working nights.

When lunching with a client, remember that if you can lie on the floor without holding on, you're not drunk.

Remember, if you're not fired with enthusiasm you'll be fired with enthusiasm.

Have you noticed how the efficiency of saleswomen varies in direct proportion to their ugliness?

Our sales manager defines zeal as a certain nervous disorder affecting young and inexperienced salesmen. Fortunately they soon get over it.

Remember, all work and no play makes Jack a dull boy and Jill a rich widow.

When it comes to giving, my firm stops at nothing. You

can do your best to make your product foolproof, but you'll never make it damn foolproof.

Our salesmen work such irregular hours that they get a free bran bonus in their pay packets.

I know a salesman who says he's the most successful in the world. He even claims to have sold Adam the first loose-leaf system.

Only the other day they put this notice up in the office. OWING TO A STAFF SHORTAGE TYPISTS WILL HANDLE SENIOR SALES MANAGEMENT BETWEEN 9 a.m. AND NOON AND SALESMEN IN THE AFTERNOON.

My boss keeps telling me that anything is possible if I only try hard enough. Personally I prefer to think anything is possible if you don't know what you're talking about.

Office notice: IN THE INTERESTS OF EFFICIENCY WILL ALL SALESMEN PLEASE TAKE ADVANTAGE OF THEIR SECRETARIES BEFORE 3 p.m.

Teamwork is essential in a sales force. That way you always have someone else to blame.

Selling is just like being a greengrocer. You have to know your onions, always dangle a carrot, and make the customer glad you've been (bean).

Confucius he say that man selling doughnuts will boast about the size of the doughnut, but the customer will consider the size of the hole.

You need to think your ideas through before you market something. The Irish may well have invented the toilet seat but it was the English who put the hole in it.

An optimistic salesman is one who believes he can sell himself to the world. A pessimistic salesman is one who thinks he already has.

Never travel without your expense account. After all, one should always take something sensational to read on a journey.

A friend of mine used to sell roller blinds but then the company was wound up.

The next time someone tells you he got rich by hard work, just try asking him whose . . .

The business of life is living — not business.

A sales conference is a gathering of people who singly do nothing and together decide that nothing can be done.

Sales meetings are where minutes are kept and hours are lost.

Looking through a brochure of hotels offering conference facilities I noticed one which read: CASUAL JACKETS ACCEPTED BUT NOT TROUSERS.

If you're buying a house, make sure you understand the language of the estate agent:
A house of old world charm No bathroom
Quiet, exclusive situation Miles from anywhere
Will benefit from improvement About to fall down
Needs refurbishing Hasn't fallen down *yet*
Ripe for development It just fell down

At a recent sales conference one of the speakers talked about Customer Rights in Advertising Policy. He called it C.R.A.P. for short, and the salesmen all agreed.

A lecherous old salesman was admitted to hospital the

other week. He lay on the sheets staring at the nurses and wishing it was the other way round.

My boss has a tray on his desk containing letters of complaint from dissatisfied customers. It's labelled OMCST — that stands for Only a Miracle Can Solve These.

Our new sales manager was like all new brooms. He made some sweeping changes and left most of us standing in the dirt.

Our sales manager is so appallingly bad at his job that his contribution to our figures last year was about the same as Arthur Scargill's to Conservative garden fêtes.

Our sales manager has the same advice for expense claims as he has for the man who delivers our parcels — 'Stuff 'em in the back passage.'

Selling any kind of goods is like selling beer. The less froth it contains, the more you'll sell.

People find some strange excuses for not buying perfectly good products. For example: The car salesman was told 'I can't aFORD it.'
The camera salesman was told 'I don't LEICA it.'
And the Paxo rep was told to stuff it . . .

Two secretaries in the typing pool were discussing the handsome new salesman.

'He dresses so smartly,' said one.

'And so quickly, too,' said the other.

Sign in a shop window. IN ORDER TO MAINTAIN THE HIGH STANDARD OF SERVICE OUR CUSTOMERS HAVE COME TO EXPECT, THIS SHOP WILL BE CLOSED ON MONDAYS, THURSDAYS AND SATURDAY AFTERNOONS.

Why is it they always have the sales when the shops are so crowded?

I've asked the chairman to let me know when to stop as I've been known to reach the end and still carry on.

COMIC SPEECHES FOR ALL OCCASIONS

Michael Kilgarriff

TAKE THE TERROR OUT OF SPEECHMAKING

The speeches people always remember are the funny ones – but that does not make them any easier to deliver. So if your progress on the rostrum or at the dinner table, by the wedding cake or at the local is dogged by trembling kneecaps and notes quivering like aspen leaves in a Force 10 gale, you need COMIC SPEECHES FOR ALL OCCASIONS.

Michael Kilgarriff, the actor, comedian, old time music hall chairman, cabaret artist and seasonal pantomime giant gives foolproof advice on all aspects of speechmaking: how to project your voice, how to handle hecklers, how to time your punch lines, which jokes to use and which subjects to avoid.

Futura Publications
Non-Fiction/Humour
0 7088 1460 3

THE BOOK OF HEROIC FAILURES

Stephen Pile

'Are you fed up with all those books telling you how to be successful? Are you dreadful at most things you try? Here at long last is a book in praise of spectacular failure and people who can't do a thing'
Namib Times

'One of the few books to make me laugh out loud'
Sunday Express

'One of the funniest and most entertaining books I have dipped into for a long time'
Country Life

'(A) splendid panorama of non-achievement'
Sunday Telegraph

'As a serious book it's a failure, as a tonic to make your ribs ache, it's a rip-roaring success'
Manchester Evening News

'A disaster'
Stephen Pile

Futura Publications
Non-Fiction
0 7088 1908 7

THE BOOK OF EXCUSES

Gyles Brandreth

A COMPLETE GUIDE TO HOW TO COME UP WITH THE PERFECT EXCUSE!

Whoever you are – a child who hasn't done his homework, a husband who arrives home later than expected, a secretary who never gets to the office on time, a zookeeper who can't persuade his pandas to breed – you need an excuse.

They don't always need to be elaborate, but they always ought to be convincing – and with Gyles Brandreth's entertaining guidance and his selection of the most amazing real-life excuses ever known – they certainly will be!

From the government spokesman who excused the fact that Britain had been left behind in the race to the moon on the grounds that we led the world in sewage treatment . . .

. . . to the Unigate milkman who told an industrial tribunal that the reason he joined the housewife in her bath was to help her rinse her empties . . .

. . . to an unemployed accountant who, when asked in court whether he had sold a £3 bag of manure for £650, replied: 'Mark-ups are normal in any profession.'

THE BOOK OF EXCUSES MEANS YOU'LL NEVER HAVE TO SAY SORRY AGAIN!

Futura Publications
Humour
0 7088 2452 8

At last!
THE OFFICIAL IRISH JOKE BOOK NO. 2

THE EAGERLY-AWAITED CLASSIC SEQUEL TO BOOKS 1, 3, AND 4

Did you know about the Irish hammer thrower given a dope test at the Olympics? He passed.

Or the sad fate of the Irish poultry farmer who went broke giving away free-range eggs?

Did you hear about the groundsman of the shinty club who thought he'd solve the drought problem by diluting the water?

Or why Paddy decided to sell his passport? He was going abroad.

At last! The Official Irish Joke Book No. 2 is here.

Futura Publications
Humour
0 7088 2669 5